This book belongs to:

Rebecca ANN Dyas

MESSAGE TO PARENTS

This book is perfect for parents and children to read aloud together. First read the story to your child. When you read the story a second time, run your finger under each line, stopping at each picture for your child to "read." Help your child to figure out the picture. If your child makes a mistake, be encouraging as you say the right word. Point out the pictures and words that are printed in the margin of each page. Soon your child will recognize the picture symbols and be "reading" aloud with you.

ISBN: 1-56288-221-X   Library of Congress Catalog Card Number: 91-77732
Printed in the U.S.A.   0 9 8 7 6 5 4 3

David and Goliath

A Read Along With Me® Book

Retold by **Laurence Schorsch**
Illustrated by **Pat Schories**

Checkerboard Press

New York

King Saul

army

valley

Long ago, during the reign of ,

the Israelites and the Philistines were at

war. One day the Philistine came to

the of Elah to fight. took the

 of Israel to meet them. 's

set up their tents on a mountain on one

side of the . The Philistines set up their

tents on the other side of the .

The greatest warrior in the Philistine  was . He came from the city of Gath. was over nine feet tall. He wore a helmet of brass on his head and a

Goliath

sword

Goliath

shield

valley

army

heavy armored coat of chain mail. He had brass armor on his shins and a plate of brass between his shoulders. He carried an enormous . His spear had a heavy brass point, and its shaft was as big as a weaver's beam. A servant walked in front of , carrying his .

 walked down into the and called to the of the Israelites, "Why

did you bring your whole ? Choose just one to fight against me. If your warrior wins, the Philistines will be your servants. But if I kill him, then the people of Israel will serve the Philistines. Send just one , and the fight will begin!"

But no came forward to fight . For when the Israelites heard speak, they were afraid.

man

David

sheep

brothers

army

King Saul

At that time there was a young shepherd named who spent his days watching over his father's . had three older in the of . One day 's father told him, "Take this grain and these ten loaves to your

in the . And take these ten

cheeses as a gift to their captain. Go and

see if they are well."

So found someone to watch the

 , and he went to the where his

  were encamped. had just

found his when appeared and

challenged the Israelites again.

"Choose a to fight against me,"

he said. "If I am killed, the Philistines will be

your servants. But if I kill your , you will

become our servants." Again the Israelites

were afraid, and no went forward to

fight .

valley

Goliath

man

David

army

brothers

sheep

Goliath

 asked, "Why is the whole of Israel afraid of this Philistine? Why does no Israelite answer his challenge?"

The oldest of 's became very angry when he heard 's words. "Why have you come here?" he asked. "Who is looking after our ? You only came here because you want to watch warriors fight a battle."

But answered, "Why are you angry? What have I done wrong? What have I said that is not true? mocks us all, and the warriors of Israel are afraid to fight him!"

Some Israelites told what

had said. called before him.

And said to , "Why do you fear

? I myself am willing to fight him."

But said, "You cannot fight .

You are only a boy who tends .

King Saul

David

King Saul

sheep

lion

bear

Goliath

army

is nine feet tall. He is a great warrior who has been fighting his whole life."

But 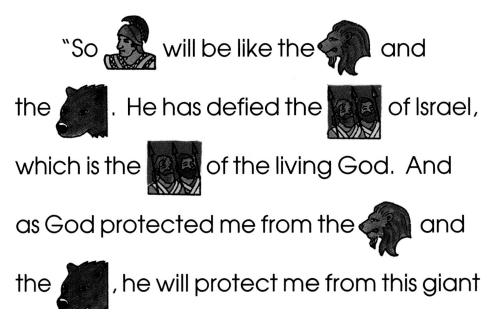 said to , "Once, when I was tending the , a and a stole a lamb from the flock. But I followed them. When the and the fought me, I killed them both and saved the lamb.

"So will be like the and the . He has defied the of Israel, which is the of the living God. And as God protected me from the and the , he will protect me from this giant Philistine."

King Saul

David

So agreed. "Go," he said, "and God be with you." And put his own armor on . He put his helmet of brass on 's head and his coat of chain mail on 's body. But  took off all the armor, saying, "I cannot wear these, for I have not yet proved myself."

 then went to a brook and found

five smooth . He put the in his

shepherd's bag. Then he took his staff in

one hand and his in the other and

walked toward the Philistine .

saw and came forward to meet him.

And 's servant also came forward,

carrying the great .

stones

sling

army

Goliath

shield

mocked because he was so young. "Do you think that I am a dog that you can beat with a staff?"

And cursed and shouted, "Come and fight. I will kill you and feed your body to the birds of the air and the beasts of the field."

Goliath

David

But  said to , "You fight with a , a spear, armor, and a . But I come to you with only 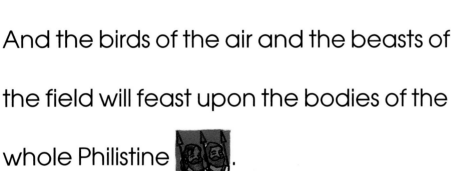 and a 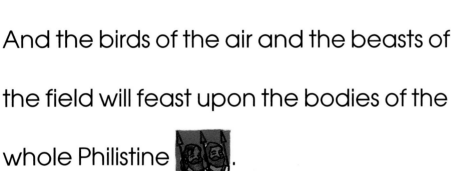 in the name of God. You defy God, but today God will give me victory over you. And the birds of the air and the beasts of the field will feast upon the bodies of the whole Philistine .

"And all the people of the earth will know that God is in Israel. They will know that God does not care who is stronger in battle. God gives victory to the righteous."

Then raised his spear, and ran toward him.

sword

shield

stones

sling

army

David

stone

sling

Goliath

sword

 took a from his bag and placed it in his . He slung the at . The hit in the forehead, and he fell to the ground. had beaten with just a and a . Then, because had no  , he took the giant's  and cut off his head.

When the Philistines saw that was

dead, they fled. And the of Israel

chased the Philistines out of the .

Now all the people of Israel loved

 . They rejoiced because he had

defeated . made the

leader of his . And when died,

 became the king of Israel.

army

valley

King Saul

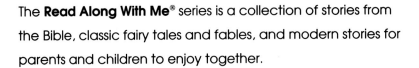

Books I have read:

☐ David and Goliath

☐ Noah's Ark

☐ The Story of Jonah

☐ The Story of Joseph

The **Read Along With Me**® series is a collection of stories from the Bible, classic fairy tales and fables, and modern stories for parents and children to enjoy together.